IMAGES
of America

FORT MOTT

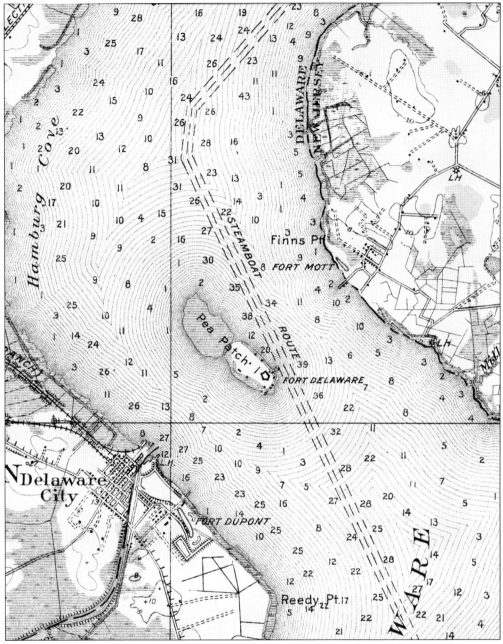

This map depicts the Delaware River as it was in 1915. Fort Mott, along with Fort Delaware on Pea Patch Island and Fort DuPont in Delaware City, Delaware, protected the ports and industry of Wilmington, Chester, Camden, and Philadelphia. (A. Grant Collection.)

ON THE COVER: In 1913, the soldiers of the 4th Company gather on one of the embankments for a photograph. The 4th Company was stationed at Fort Mott from 1911 until 1914. (Drummond Collection.)

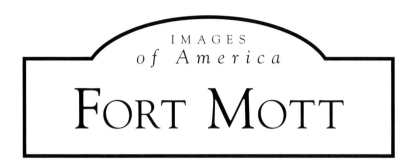

IMAGES
of America

FORT MOTT

Andres G. Grant

ARCADIA
PUBLISHING

Published by Arcadia Publishing
Charleston, South Carolina

Printed in the United States of America

Library of Congress Control Number: 2012944906

For all general information, please contact Arcadia Publishing:
Telephone 843-853-2070
Fax 843-853-0044
E-mail sales@arcadiapublishing.com
For customer service and orders:
Toll-Free 1-888-313-2665

Visit us on the Internet at www.arcadiapublishing.com

For Col. Andres J. Garcia and Robert H. Grant Sr.

CONTENTS

ACKNOWLEDGMENTS

In its time as an Army post and later as a state park, countless soldiers, dependents, visitors, and staff have walked the grounds of Fort Mott. The donations and loans from families who once called Fort Mott home have helped to make this book possible. I would like to thank the families of Pvt. James Drummond, Sgt. Fred Klein, and M.Sgt. Harry Darsney, whose families' photographs and images are displayed in this book. I would also like to thank B.W. Smith, Stephen Turner Jr., Vince Turner, and Chris Zeeman for use of their collection of Fort Mott images and also Vince Turner II and Sara and Larry Winchell with helping edit text. I would also like to especially thank my wife, Wynne, for all her help and understanding as I put this book together.

INTRODUCTION

As far back as the time of George Washington, it was known that the confluence of the Delaware Bay and the Delaware River would provide the best location to build fortifications to protect the city of Philadelphia and surrounding industry. With this in mind, in 1837, land was purchased by the federal government in a part of New Jersey known as Finns Point. Formerly colonized by Finland, this area of land jutted out into the Delaware River toward Pea Patch Island, where a fort was already under construction.

However, it was not until the 1870s that technological advances made the construction of fortifications on the site a viable option. The weaponry advancements that took place during the Civil War made large masonry fortifications, such as those on Pea Patch Island, obsolete. Therefore, in order to bolster the defensive capabilities of the Delaware River, the Army decided to build fortifications on both sides of the river across from Pea Patch Island. The original plan for the fortification at Finns Point included an 11-gun battery, but due to storm damage and cuts to the defense budget, only five of the gun emplacements were ever completed.

The next construction project at Finns Point was part of a new system of fortifications planned for the defenses of the United States. Later termed Endicott fortifications, these sites utilized all the newest technology in construction and armament. Consisting of massive gun batteries constructed of concrete and steel and covered with earth to conceal their locations from enemy ships, this style of fortification was America's front line of defense until World War II.

Construction began at Finns Point in the late 1890s, and in 1897, the site was renamed Fort Mott for Gen. Gershom Mott, a Civil War hero from New Jersey. Construction of the fort was completed by 1900; at that time, the fort was at the cutting edge of military might. Fully garrisoned with troops throughout World War I, as many as 400 men were stationed at Fort Mott during this time. In 1922, with the "War To End All Wars" over, the bulk of the Army troops were ordered out of Fort Mott, leaving engineers and caretakers to maintain the fort and its buildings.

In the quiet years between the wars, Fort Mott was never really quiet. From the caretakers going about their daily routines to National Guard soldiers arriving for their annual maneuvers, Fort Mott was always abuzz with activity.

In the mid-1930s, with hostilities again beginning to boil over in Europe, the Army decided that Fort Mott's infrastructure should be upgraded in case the guns were ever called back into action. The telephone system, which had been mainly dormant, was upgraded, as was the fire control on site. When war did break out on December 7, 1941, Fort Mott had the 12-inch guns of Battery Arnold at the ready.

Fortunately, war never made it to the continental United States, and Fort Mott was not needed. In 1944, the Army abandoned the fort, and once the war was over, it put the property up for sale. In 1947, the State of New Jersey purchased all 104 acres for $14,000 with the intention of turning the land into a state park. On June 24, 1951, Fort Mott State Park opened to the public with great fanfare. In the 60 years since the park opened, there has been a renewed interest in the site's history, not only as regards the local community but as one of the best-preserved Endicott fortifications in the United States.

One

THE BATTERY
AT FINNS POINT

With the advancements in military technology and the increased industrial capability in post–Civil War America, the government realized the need to update and improve the nation's defenses in order to secure the country's future. As part of what was later called the "Endicott period" of fortification construction, Fort Mott, on Finns Point, New Jersey, and Fort DuPont, just south of Delaware City, Delaware, were built to bolster the defensive line that began with Fort Delaware on Pea Patch Island. Originally referred to as the Battery at Finns Point, Fort Mott was officially named on December 17, 1897, for Civil War general Gershom Mott. By the time the fort was completed, it consisted of five gun batteries containing 12 guns in total. The fort's Battery Arnold could fire a 1,270-pound projectile over eight miles downriver toward any enemy vessel. Fort Mott was the eastern anchor of a respectable line of forts across the Delaware.

With the completion of the concrete fortifications, the large breach-loading rifles and their carriages are unloaded from a barge onto the wharf. At the time Fort Mott was constructed, the roads leading to the military reservation were often considered impassible, and most construction material arrived via the Delaware River. (National Archives.)

This photograph shows the lower part of the large bearing for the gun of Battery Arnold' Emplacement 2 being prepared to be connected to the gun block. The roller bearings enable the gun to be easily moved or traversed from side to side. (National Archives.)

The upper section of the bearing race is being lowered upon the cylindrical rollers. It was of the upmost importance that the bearing race be absolutely level. (National Archives.)

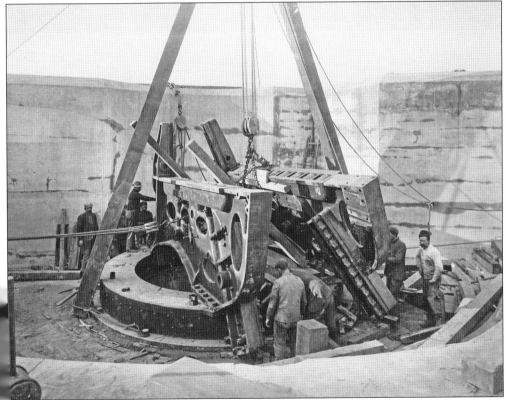

With the help of block and tackle, the large sides of the carriage are placed upon the bearing, and the arms that will raise and lower the rifled barrel of the gun are attached to the carriage. The counterweight, which made possible the quick raising of the gun into firing position, would be attached to the arms as well. The counterweights for one of Battery Arnold's guns weighed 20,000 pounds. (National Archives.)

The carriage is now complete and ready to accept the barrel. The night before this photograph was taken, snow had fallen and is visible on the wood blocking. (National Archives.)

A large ramp is built to haul the barrel onto the gun deck and then onto the carriage. A steam engine used to help pull the barrel into place is visible in the center right of the photograph. In the background, entrances to Battery Krayenbuhl are visible, as is the rear earthen mound, or *parados*, that would run the entire length of the gun line upon completion. (National Archives.)

Slowly, the 12-inch barrel is hoisted up the ramp to the gun deck. In the lower right of the photograph, the small railway that ran from the end of the pier all the way behind the main gun line is visible. As ammunition was unloaded at the wharf, the railway made it much easier to move the heavy projectiles and powder to the magazines. (National Archives.)

The barrel is now attached to the carriage, and men from the Ordnance Department work on completing the gun. (National Archives.)

Battery Arnold's Gun 2 is now ready for action. A worker stands to the rear of the gun behind an ammunition cart while the gun is in loading position. This three-wheeled cart was used to move the projectiles and gunpowder from the hoist to the gun. Also of note is the elevated stand that allowed the crew to see over the protective concrete wall. (National Archives.)

Battery Arnold's Gun 2 is seen here in firing position. The large counterweights, now located beneath the gun, helped to lift the gun, allowing it to fire from above the protective concrete wall. Once fired, the recoil caused the gun to lower back to the loading position. This raising and lowering of the gun is why they were called "disappearing guns." (National Archives.)

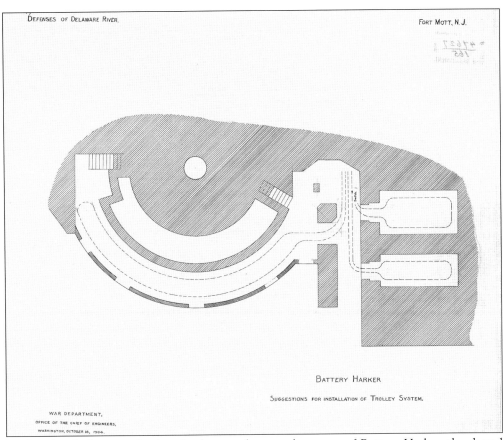

BATTERY HARKER

SUGGESTIONS FOR INSTALLATION OF TROLLEY SYSTEM.

WAR DEPARTMENT,
OFFICE OF THE CHIEF OF ENGINEERS,
WASHINGTON, OCTOBER 18, 1904.

In this sketch showing the interior layout of an emplacement of Battery Harker, the dotted lines represent the proposed placement of overhead trolley tracks to be used to move the heavy projectiles around the lower level of the emplacement. (National Archives.)

Emplacement 2's 10-inch disappearing gun at Battery Harker is seen here in firing position. This image shows the original configuration of the emplacement. It was later determined that there was not enough room to load the guns efficiently, so in 1908, platform extensions were added. (A. Grant Collection.)

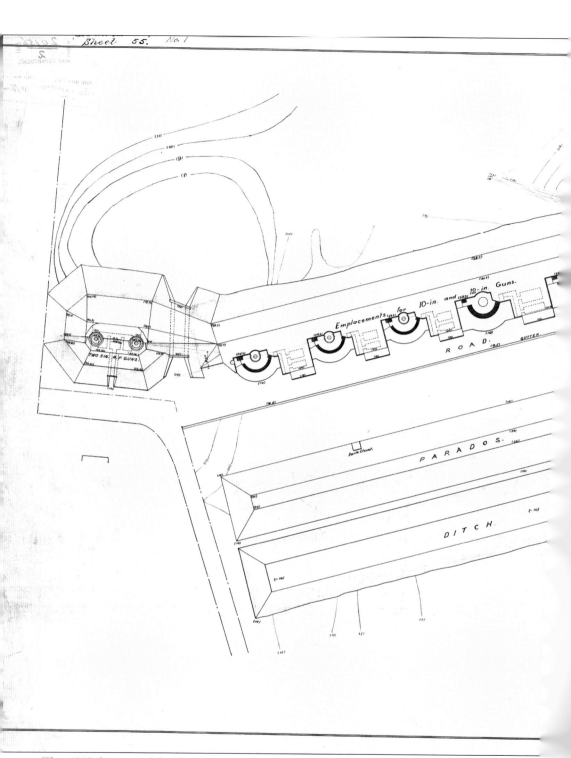

This 1897 drawing of the Battery at Finns Point shows the proposed locations of emplacements for five-inch rapid-fire guns. This drawing shows, excepting some minor changes, how Fort Mott was eventually laid out. When completed, the gun batteries would be named, from left to

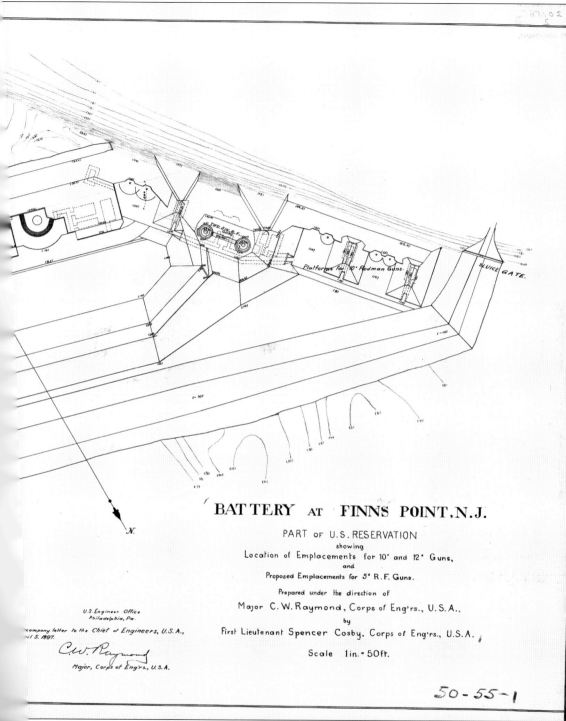

BATTERY AT **FINN'S POINT, N.J.**

PART OF U.S. RESERVATION

showing

Location of Emplacements for 10" and 12" Guns,

and

Proposed Emplacements for 5" R.F. Guns.

Prepared under the direction of

Major C.W. Raymond, Corps of Eng'rs., U.S.A.,

by

First Lieutenant Spencer Cosby, Corps of Eng'rs., U.S.A.

Scale 1in. = 50ft.

U.S. Engineer Office
Philadelphia, Pa.

accompany letter to the Chief of Engineers, U.S.A.,
April 5. 1897.

C.W. Raymond

Major, Corps of Eng'rs., U.S.A.

N.

Platforms for 10" Rodman Guns.

SLUICE GATE.

50-55-1

ight, Battery Gregg, Battery Harker, Battery Arnold, Battery Edwards, and Battery Krayenbuhl.
National Archives.)

Brig. Gen. Charles G. Harker, US Volunteers, served with distinction during the Civil War and was killed in action on June 27, 1864, at the Battle of Kennesaw Mountain in Georgia. General Harker was a native of Swedesboro, New Jersey. Battery Harker was named in his honor on October 9, 1902, in General Order No. 105. (National Archives.)

. Col. Lewis G. Arnold, 2nd US Artillery, and brigadier general, US Volunteers, served with
stinction in the Florida War, the Mexican War, and the Civil War. Battery Arnold was named
his honor on October 9, 1902, in General Order No. 105. (National Archives.)

Maj. Gen. Gershom Mott, US Volunteers, was born on April 7, 1822, in Lamberton, New Jersey. A veteran of the Mexican War and the Civil War, General Mott was known for his bravery in battle and ability to lead troops. After the Civil War, Mott held numerous titles within state government until the time of his death in 1884. Fort Mott was named in December 1897 in his honor. (National Archives.)

Two

FORT MOTT

For over 20 years, Fort Mott was on the front line of the nation's homeland defense. With guns that could reach out almost 10 miles downriver, and working in conjunction with Fort DuPont, Fort Delaware, and other forts around the nation, the fort was never attacked by an enemy force. Fort Mott was designed like many other Army posts of the period with a large parade ground at the its center. The enlisted men's barracks were at the top, while the officers' and noncommissioned officers' quarters faced each other on opposite sides of the parade ground.

During down time, the soldiers participated in many activities, such as baseball, basketball, and football, and for the officers, Fort Mott had its own clay tennis court. A library, which doubled as a schoolhouse, was provided for the soldiers and their children. In many respects, Fort Mott was its own small town, offering most things a soldier could want, including a post exchange to buy dry goods and a commissary to buy food. With either a short wagon ride to the city of Salem or a boat ride to Delaware City, Delaware, the soldiers could easily access supplies that could not be found on post.

Always ready for action, the soldiers at Fort Mott constantly drilled on the guns. However, after two practice projectiles from Fort DuPont landed in Salem, New Jersey, in 1904, Fort Mott's soldiers were required to go to Fort Monroe, Virginia, for large-caliber practice. In the years following initial construction, the fort underwent many upgrades, such as platform extensions on Battery Harker and Battery Arnold, which helped to make Fort Mott more efficient than originally designed. When the United States entered World War I, the fort's housing reached maximum capacity, and temporary housing had to be built to accommodate the increase in personnel. When the "War To End All Wars" concluded in 1918, the Army began construction of a new fort farther south on the Delaware Bay that utilized the advancements in military technology developed during the war. Fort Saulsbury, near Milford, Delaware, could fend off enemy vessels while they were in the Delaware Bay, before they even entered the Delaware River and the reach of Fort Mott's guns. As a result, Fort Mott and the other forts of the upper Delaware River defenses found themselves reduced to caretaker status.

This patriotic postcard is like many others that were available to the soldiers at the post exchange. This card was sent on August 26, 1908, by a soldier at Fort Mott. (A. Grant Collection.)

Fort Mott, N. J.

This period postcard view of the post headquarters and officers' row is looking east on Cemetery Road. Originally, the flagpole was located in the street, directly in front of the post headquarters. It was later moved to the parade ground. The building on the left is barracks that were used by the men who built the fortifications and buildings. This building would later be used as a commissary. (A. Grant Collection.)

Headquarters and Officer's Residences, Fort Mott, New Jersey

Range Finder, Fort Mott, N. J.

This two-story, glass-topped tower rises 53 feet into the air and once commanded excellent views of ships traveling on the Delaware River. Originally, the lower floor contained azimuth instruments for sighting ships, a meteorological station, and a plotting room. Later, a plotting room was established on the parados, and the extra space in the tower was used for three telephone booths for communication. (A. Grant Collection.)

These blueprints for the "Tower and Instrument Room for the Range and Position Finders Battery for 10-inch Guns" show the makeup of the tower that stands in front of the guardhouse. Built in 1903, this two-story tower acted as the "eyes" for Battery Harker and originally housed a plotting room and weather station. (National Archives.)

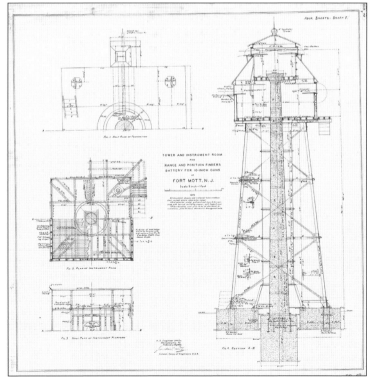

23

Military guards line up in front of the guardhouse. Built in 1903 next to the moat, the guardhouse was capable of imprisoning 12 soldiers. The building has served many purposes during its lifespan: guardhouse, mess hall, quarters, and, currently, the Fort Mott State Park office. (A. Grant Collection.)

This period postcard of Officers' Row is looking west on Cemetery Road. Officers' Row consisted of five buildings, two of which were duplexes. The last building on the row was the post headquarters. The cannonballs in small stacks in front of the buildings are 15-inch Rodman projectiles that were left over from the original 1870s construction. The cannonballs adorned many walkways around the buildings on post. (A. Grant Collection.)

The 42nd Company Coast Artillery was stationed at Fort Mott from 1901 until 1911, when it was transferred to Fort Mills in the Philippine Islands. This photograph was taken with the unit's barracks in the background. The company officers are sitting in the middle of the front row and are distinguished by their swords. (Vince Turner Collection.)

Initially the post's guardhouse, this building was later converted into the Fort Mott library and times also served as the post's schoolhouse for children of soldiers and officers. After the Army abandoned Fort Mott, this building was moved across the street from the fort and converted to private residence. (A. Grant Collection.)

Guard House, Fort Mott, N. J.

In this view of the guardhouse, a soldier is seen standing to the left of the porch and another soldier is on the porch. The building visible in the background on the right is a quartermaster storehouse, whose foundation is visible today along Cemetery Road. (A. Grant Collection.)

One of the first buildings erected at Fort Mott was Building 5 (officers' quarters). It stood directly to the rear of Battery Gregg and was continuously used as family housing until the fort was abandoned. When the State of New Jersey purchased Fort Mott, the building was sold and moved off the park property to be used as a private residence. This photograph from 1904 shows Building 5 in its original location with the post headquarters and flagpole visible to the right rear of the structure. (National Archives.)

Buildings 4 and 6, officers' quarters (shown here), consisted of two dwellings for officers assigned to Fort Mott. All of the buildings of Officers' Row, except the post headquarters, were floated across the Delaware River to Fort DuPont in the 1930s. Of the five buildings moved, this officers' quarters is the only building still standing today. (National Archives.)

This rare photograph shows the 1908 Fort Mott football team in Salem, New Jersey. Sports and athletic activities were an important aspect of a soldier's life at Fort Mott. In addition to football, baseball was extremely popular with the troops. The fort also had a clay tennis court for officers located next to the two-story tower. (Fort Mott State Park.)

Located near the guardhouse, Building 10 (the ordnance warehouse) was built in 1901 and had a storage capacity of over 16,000 cubic feet. Today, the building serves as the park's museum and gift shop. (National Archives.)

Building 18, the pump house, was used to provide water pressure to the buildings on post. The building, constructed of corrugated steel, was torn down in 1932. It stood near what is now the park's maintenance shop. (National Archives.)

138TH Co. C.A.C, FORT MOTT, N.J.

The 138th Company Coast Artillery poses for this winter photograph. The troops are all wearing their heavy woolen overcoats. (Stephen Turner Jr. Collection.)

Fort Mott's post flagpole was located on the parade ground directly in front of the post headquarters. One of the two barracks buildings is directly behind the flagpole. To the left of the flagpole is a stack of cannonballs, which remained in that location until the Army abandoned Fort Mott. (National Archives.)

In this 1917 postcard image of the main batteries, taken from atop Battery Krayenbuhl, the coal shed for the generating room is visible to the lower left. Electricity at Fort Mott was originally generated via these steam-powered generators. In 1918, new gasoline-powered General Electric 25-kilowatt generators were installed. (Vince Turner Collection.)

The 4th Company Coast Artillery's baseball team poses for a photograph in 1912 after a game at Fort DuPont, Delaware. The units of soldiers assigned to the forts that comprised the harbor defenses of the Delaware often competed against each other in sports. Each team's uniform would be distinctive to the unit. The 4th Company's uniform read "4th Co. C.A.C." (Stephen Turner Jr. Collection.)

On this period postcard, the following building labels have been handwritten, from left to right: "Officer's Row, 7 fine houses," "Commissary," "119th Co CAC," "In under those trees is the National Cemetery," "42nd Co CAC," "138th Co in camp," and "Just out of sight Hospital and staff Houses." On the back, the card reads, "The fort is over back of the Officer's Row. They are not allowed to photograph the fort." (A. Grant Collection.)

rt Mott's two main barracks buildings, located on the western edge of the parade ground, uld each house 107 men. Each barracks had sleeping, eating, toilet, and shower facilities. (A. ant Collection.)

In this photograph of Fort Mott's main gate, looking west on Cemetery Road, large granite columns flank each side of the entrance to the military post. The building to the left is a single-family officer's house originally reserved for field-grade officers (the rank of major and above). (A. Grant Collection.)

This photograph, labeled "Willow Lane," was taken looking south from the post headquarter toward Battery Gregg. The front porch of the post library is barely visible on the left, an decorative cannonballs can be seen on both sides of the sidewalk. The grounds of the po were meticulously maintained with pride by the soldiers who called Fort Mott home. (A Grant Collection.)

In this photograph of the guardhouse, the passage of time is evidenced by the electrical and telephone wires running overhead and by the trees in front that are no longer mere saplings. The building was heated by a coal-fired boiler, and the open coal chute to the basement is visible. Today, this building is Fort Mott State Park's office, and the area that once held the jail cells now contains the visitor restrooms. (A. Grant Collection.)

oldiers of the 4th Company Coast Artillery gather for a game of baseball on the parade ground. he post hospital is just out of sight on the left, while just visible through the trees to the left are e two noncommissioned staff officers' duplex quarters. (Stephen Turner Jr. Collection.)

James Drummond joined the Army in Ohio and was assigned to Fort Mott. In this photograph, he is wearing a blue five-button sack coat, likely from the 1870s. Coast Artillery soldiers were regularly not given the latest uniforms. (Drummond Collection.)

In October 1913, the 138th Company Coast Artillery Corps was sent to Fort Monroe in Virginia for target practice. This photograph shows the unit waiting for food while encamped in Phoenix, Maryland. James Drummond is labeled "Pop." (Drummond Collection.)

In this novelty photograph, a soldier of the 4th Company Coast Artillery Corps appears to be riding the "Water Wagon." In the early 1900s, riding the water wagon meant that an individual was abstaining from drinking alcohol. (Drummond Collection.)

A LONG RIDE TOO.

This 1913 image depicts some of the high jinks that soldiers in camp would get into while awaiting orders. The rifles the soldiers are holding are 1903 Springfield rifles with affixed bayonets. James Drummond is visible to the far right, leaning on a tent support. (Drummond Collection.)

James Drummond (left) and another soldier stand near a communication niche at a disappearing gun emplacement during target practice. James Drummond is wearing an EE-70 headset hooked into a battery commander's telephone. As information was relayed via telephone to the soldiers, the data could be recorded on the deflection board, shown to the left of the telephone, and the time range board, shown to the right of the image. (Drummond Collection.)

The men of the 4th Company Coast Artillery Corps pose for a photograph around a six-pound cannon on September 1, 1913, while encamped for target practice. The six-pounder was used as an anti-personnel weapon at seacoast forts in the event that enemy forces were able to land infantry troops. (Drummond Collection.)

In this period photograph, Fort Mott's 4th Company Coast Artillery is encamped at Fort Monroe, Virginia. While at target practice, a unit brought everything it needed from its home duty station. James Drummond is standing in front of his tent, the third from the left. (Drummond Collection.)

It was common for professional photographers to come to encampments and take photographs of the troops. These photographs would then be made into postcards, which the troops could send back to family and friends. In this postcard, the men of the 4th Company are photographed during some down time. James Drummond is standing, second from the left. (Drummond Collection.)

Men of the 4th Company stop for a photograph on the parade ground before going to chow. The company's mascot is in the center of the front row. Very often, units would have some sort of mascot; at Fort Mott, the mascot of choice was a dog. (Drummond Collection.)

In this period photograph, the new uniform for the 4th Company Coast Artillery Corp baseball team is pictured. The new uniform (left) is white with the unit design now a "4 inside of "CO," which stood for company. The old uniform simply had "4th Co. C.A.C" on i (Drummond Collection.)

Men of the 4th Company Coast Artillery Corps are seen posing on their disappearing gun while it was in firing position. If this gun were not returned to loading position through firing, the crew would be required to perform the arduous task of cranking it down by hand. (Drummond Collection.)

In this photograph, soldiers of Fort Mott's 4th Company root for their baseball team as plays Fort DuPont's 45th Company on the baseball field located on the parade ground. (Drummond Collection.)

Ships pass in Salem Cove, off the shores of Fort Mott. As men stationed in the observation post would look out at the river's traffic, their first sign that a vessel was underway would be plumes of dark smoke. When the ship neared, it was up to the soldiers to identify it. (Drummond Collection.)

This period postcard shows the guard mount forming up on the parade ground with the post hospital in the background. Individuals were identified on the back of the postcard as follows: "I am the fourth man counting either way, Lieutenant Eglin is inspecting the guards. The three men to the left are the buglers. The lone soldier to the right is the Sergeant Major." (Vince Turner Collection.)

This photograph of the two barracks looks toward the quartermaster storehouse on Cemetery Road. From the top porch of each of the buildings, laundry is hung out to dry. The barracks were dismantled in the mid-1930s. (A. Grant Collection.)

Building 28 and 29, noncommissioned staff officers' quarters, and the one built next to it, Building 25 and 26, were designed as duplexes. Originally lighted with mineral oil, these buildings still stand on the northern edge of the parade ground, awaiting restoration. (National Archives.)

In this photograph, soldiers are practicing using signal flags, or "wig wags." The type of signal flag the soldiers are using dates back to the Civil War. Messages were transmitted to others by waving the signal flag back and forth in a set pattern, which would form letters and numbers. (A. Grant Collection.)

This photograph of the post flagpole was taken from the porch of the post headquarters. The soldiers of Fort Mott gathered in the morning to raise the American flag and in the evening to lower the flag for retreat. The white horn located near the base was for the bugler. (A. Grant Collection.)

As shown in this photograph of the post hospital, a porch was added to the wing on the left, and shutters were added to the windows. The hospital would remain at Fort Mott until it was dismantled in the mid-1930s. (A. Grant Collection.)

This aerial photograph of Fort Mott from the early 1920s shows the numerous farms that once surrounded the Army post. The wharf can be seen jutting out into the Delaware River. Many of these farms were destroyed when the protective dyke failed in the mid-1930s and the river permanently flooded the fields. (National Archives.)

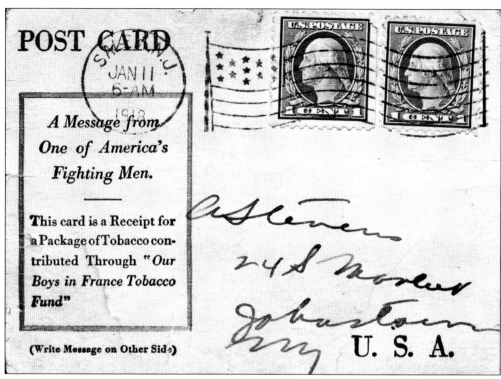

POST CARD

A Message from One of America's Fighting Men.

This card is a Receipt for a Package of Tobacco contributed Through "*Our Boys in France Tobacco Fund*"

(Write Message on Other Side)

This postcard, sent on January 11, 1918, reads: "With much thanks and appreciation. I enjoyed the very thoughtful gifts, you know I am grateful for them. Sgt. Vernon Knox C.A. Co. N.A. Fort Mott. Salem N.J." (Both, Vince Turner Collection.)

In this photograph, labeled "Birds-eye View, Fort Mott, N.J.," many of the buildings that once made up Fort Mott are clearly visible. This photograph was taken from atop the parados. (Vince Turner Collection.)

Projectiles from Battery Harker's magazines are placed on the sidewalk to the rear of the emplacements for inspection and cleaning. At least yearly, the projectiles were taken out of the magazine and were cleaned and painted. These projectiles appear to have just been painted. (Vince Turner Collection.)

During World War I, the Army grew larger than it had been in many years. To help accommodate all of the new soldiers at Fort Mott, two new barracks were built. This photograph shows Building 107 (barracks) as it stood in 1918. (National Archives.)

In addition to enlisted men, an increase of officers was also experienced at Fort Mott during World War I. Small quarters were built to house the officers and their families while stationed at Fort Mott. This photograph shows Building 101 (officers' quarters). An identical quarters stood next to it. (National Archives.)

The new barracks erected to house the growing enlisted population at Fort Mott were built without plumbing. All of the toilet and shower facilities for the new barracks were located within Building 104 (lavatory), shown here. (National Archives.)

With more men being stationed at Fort Mott, more equipment and supplies were needed to support them. Building 105 (storehouse) was built adjacent to all of the buildings erected on Fort Mott during World War I. (National Archives.)

Along with the need for additional space to store the soldiers' equipment, additional facilities were needed to feed them. Building 103, the mess hall, was designed to serve both of the two new barracks. All of the buildings erected during the World War I "emergency" were torn down within a decade. (National Archives.)

This photograph of the post hospital was taken during World War I. Barely visible behind the bushes in front of the hospital are the new enlisted barracks and officers' quarters. (Fort Mott State Park.)

Erected in 1897, Building 30 had many functions over its lifespan. Able to seat 109 men at a time for meals, this building was moved at one point closer to the large barracks. After it was a mess hall, Building 30 served as a commissary storehouse and post exchange. (National Archives.)

Building 17 (hose house), erected at a cost of $146.20, could store two hose carts that could be used in case of fire. Originally, Building 17 sat next to the barracks, but it was moved next to the guardhouse in the 1930s. This building was later moved by the park service to the base of the wharf. (National Archives.)

Built in 1903, Building 23 (the coal shed) had a capacity of 250 tons. All heat in the buildings came from either coal stoves or coal-fired boilers. The coal shed was located along Cemetery Road and remained standing until the late 1930s. (National Archives.)

The original wharf was built in 1873–1874 to support the construction of the 11-gun battery that was to be built on site. Building 20 (wharf) was reconstructed by the Army in 1905 and then by the State of New Jersey in 1996 and 1997. (National Archives.)

During World War I, many coastal forts saw some of their armament dismounted and shipped to Europe for use by field artillery or railway artillery. Fort Mott was ordered to dismount the guns of Battery Harker and prepare them for shipment. Fortunately, the order to ship the barrels never came, and the barrels were remounted on their carriages, as this photograph depicts. (Fort Mott State Park.)

This aerial photograph provides an outstanding view of the layout of Fort Mott, with all of the post buildings still standing. In the well-manicured parade ground, the baseball diamond is visible. (National Archives.)

Three

CARETAKERS

With the conclusion of World War I and the ever-advancing improvements to seacoast artillery, Fort Mott was no longer at the cutting edge of military might. The completion of Fort Saulsbury in Delaware meant that an enemy attack by sea could be halted in the Delaware Bay before it ever reached Fort Mott's field of fire. In 1922, the main garrison of regular Army troops was moved from Fort Mott, leaving behind only the Army engineers and a small detachment of Coast Artillery caretakers. These men were tasked with the maintenance of the fortifications, buildings, and grounds so that the fort would be ready should the next war come to the shores of the United States. For almost 20 years, the caretakers and their families lived on the Army post, maintaining the infrastructure and big guns. Many of these caretakers raised their families during the interwar period.

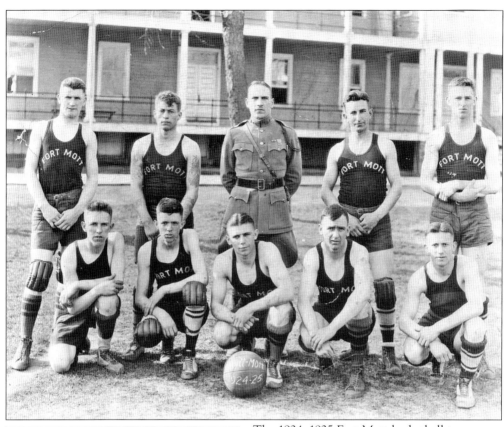

The 1924–1925 Fort Mott basketball team poses in front of the barracks. A first lieutenant and veteran of World War I stands in uniform in the back row. With fewer men to choose from, smaller team sports like basketball were more popular with the soldiers. (Sullivan Collection.)

Two soldiers from Battery E of the 7th Coast Artillery have their photograph taken on the beach along the Delaware River. Battery E was assigned to Fort Mott, Fort DuPont, and Fort Delaware to maintain the fortifications and armament. (Watterson Clement Collection.)

A soldier and his wife sit on the beach at Fort Mott in front of the seawall. The building in the background once stood at the base of the wharf and was a storehouse for the engineers. This building was later moved next to the stable. (Watterson Clement Collection.)

Two women push baby carriages between Battery Gregg and Building 5. With less restrictions due to a greatly reduced number of soldiers stationed at the fort, the caretakers and their families were able to move around the site with more freedom than would have been possible with the full compliment of troops assigned to Fort Mott. (Watterson Clement Collection.)

William "Tubby" Watterson and Mary Watterson's school pictures from 1931 and 1930 are shown here. Mary was born at Fort Mott on December 3, 1922. Mary and Tubby's father arrived at Fort Mott in 1921 as a cook for Company A, 3rd Regiment of Engineers. (Both, Watterson Clement Collection.)

Sgt. Harry Darsney and his sister Anna pose for a photograph in 1938 behind his quarters at Fort Mott. Harry Darsney entered the Army in 1924 and was the last sergeant assigned to Fort Mott. (Darsney Collection.)

Battery Arnold's Gun 1 is shown in this 1930s photograph. The caretakers were tasked with maintaining the large guns so they could be called back into service if the country ever needed them for defense. Fortunately, the guns never had to fire at an enemy. (Watterson Clement Collection.)

Doris Darsney stands in front of a pile of cannonballs in 1940. These cannonballs are left over from the 1870s construction. Over the years, the cannonballs sank into the ground so much that only the tops of the lowest level of cannonballs were still visible. The vast emptiness of the once-busy parade ground lies in the background. (Darsney Collection.)

Bernice (in front) and Dottie Darsney stand behind the old post library, which was located next to their quarters. The parados is visible across the road from the library. (Darsney Collection.)

Jim and Dottie Darsney play near the quarters that had once been the post headquarters. When many of the other buildings were either moved to Fort DuPont or dismantled, the headquarters was turned into family housing. Later, the family moved into Building 5, behind Battery Gregg. (Darsney Collection.)

In this 1943 photograph, Bernice Darsney is held by her grandfather Peter Zodorsney. The eastern fire control tower and old post headquarters are in the background. (Darsney Collection.)

In this photograph, the Darsney children line up on the parade ground in front of the quarters. Shown here are, from left to right, Harry "Bunny" Darsney Jr., Paul "Babe" Darsney, Dottie Darsney, and Jimmy Darsney. (Darsney Collection.)

Bernice Darsney wears her father's uniform hat while he holds her behind their home on Fort Mott in 1943. By 1943, Fort Mott was slated for abandonment by the Army, and the remaining guns in Battery Arnold were being scrapped. (Darsney Collection.)

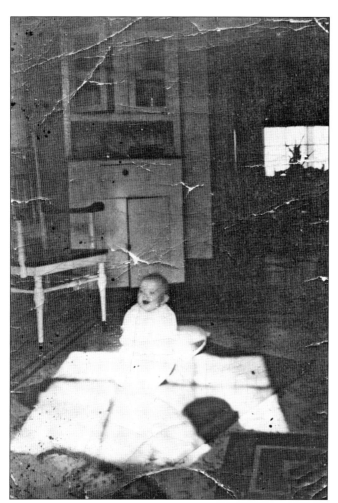

In this rare photograph of the interior of quarters at Fort Mott, Elmer Darsney takes in the sun's rays. Elmer is photographed in one of the back rooms on the first floor of Building 9 while it was being used as family housing. (Darsney Collection.)

Soldiers stationed at Fort Mott pose in front of one of Battery Arnold's large 12-inch disappearing guns. It was the job of the caretakers to make sure that all the guns and equipment were kept in working order in case they were ever needed. (Darsney Collection.)

Harry Darsney Jr. holds up his sister Doris as brothers Joe (left) and Jimmy look on. This photograph was taken in front of Building 25, which was one of the noncommissioned officers' quarters on the north side of the parade ground. (Darsney Collection.)

One of the projects that the caretakers completed was the lining of the post generating room with corrugated asbestos sheeting. Seen here on the walls and ceiling, the asbestos helped to keep moisture off the electrical equipment by channeling any drips from the ceiling to the walls, where it would run into a gutter. (Fort Mott State Park.)

This photograph from the eastern fire control tower shows an unobstructed view of the river and the field of fire for Battery Arnold and Battery Harker. Building 5 can be seen to the left, and Battery Gregg and the battery commander's station are in the center of the photograph. (National Archives.)

Soldiers of the 70th Engineers take a photograph with 18-month-old Bernice Darsney in front of her house in 1942. This house now sits across the road from the park and is currently being restored. (Darsney Collection.)

As part of reestablishing the ability of the large guns to fire into the Delaware River, many of the large trees that had grown up since 1922, when Fort Mott's garrison of troops was reduced to just a handful of soldiers, had to be cut down. The western fire control tower is clearly visible rising above the landscape. (National Archives.)

Camouflaging the gun emplacements was very important to coastal fortifications. The photograph above shows what existed, and the drawing below shows how, with proper camouflage, Fort Mott could disappear into the landscape. The artist proposes in the sketch below of the same area that the fire control towers be made to look like water towers to help hide their true purpose. (Both, National Archives.)

In this set of camouflaging ideas, the battery commander's station on Battery Gregg in the photograph above is modified to look more like a house, and the eastern fire control tower is made to look like a water tower, as depicted in the artist's rendering of the area. (Both, National Archives.)

Although many trees had just been cut down around the fortifications, the artist proposes planting trees behind the main gun line and building a "cottage-looking" structure on the parados. In the conceptual drawing below, the peace magazine is almost invisible. (Both, National Archives.)

In the last artist rendition of how Fort Mott could attain better concealment, the battery commander's station would be modified to look like a shack instead of the flat-roofed angular box. (Both, National Archives.)

This photograph shows the wharf and river from the eastern fire control tower. With the United States's entry into World War II, ship traffic to England picked up markedly on the Delaware River. This increase in shipping caused the seawall to fail due to all of the wake generated by the ships. Soldiers, with the help of the WPA, had to constantly repair the seawall along the river. (National Archives.)

From the eastern fire control tower, trees have begun to restrict the view toward the western tower. The moat and parados can easily be recognized in the area between the towers. (National Archives.)

The end of Battery Arnold Emplacement 2 does not come in battle but by the hands of a torch. In this photograph, the entire barrel has been cut in half, while the carts once used to move the heavy projectiles sit under their protective concrete cover. (Casemate Museum.)

This photograph shows another sad view of one of Battery Arnold's gun tubes being cut down the center. The spiral pattern that made up the tube's rifling is visible inside the half-gun barrel. As the gun was cut up, parts were tossed over the side. A pile of gun parts is visible at ground level behind the worker. (Casemate Museum.)

A special rig with a torch was made to help cut up the barrels quickly. By the time the guns of Battery Arnold were cut up for scrap, they were already almost 50 years old. The gun of Emplacement 2 was in such poor shape due to its age that the army believed if it ever needed to be fired with a full charge, it would only be able to be fired once and then would be rendered unserviceable. (Casemate Museum.)

Another view shows the rig that helped cut up Fort Mott's guns. The soldier on the left uses a hand-pump fire extinguisher, marked "Fort DuPont," to put out any stray embers. By the time the guns were cut up for scrap, only seven soldiers were assigned to Fort Mott. (Casemate Museum.)

One of Battery Arnold's large gun tubes is being lifted by a crane after a third of the barrel has already been cut off. By 1944, all of the large-caliber guns had been removed from the three forts that once helped to keep enemy vessels from attacking Philadelphia. (Casemate Museum.)

The end has now reached Battery Arnold. All of the battery's guns have met their end and are being hauled off to the scrap yard. Two shell carts as well as a subcaliber platform can be seen under the protection of the concrete overhang. The crane is now hauling gun parts out of Arnold's Emplacement 1. (Casemate Museum.)

The old post headquarters had been turned into family housing when the lack of space forced the soldiers to repurpose the building. For some time, Sergeant Darsney and his family called it home. After they moved to another building, the plan was to convert it into bachelors' quarters. (Darsney Collection.)

Four

FORT MOTT STATE PARK

The year 1947 marked a change of ownership for the former defender of the Delaware when the State of New Jersey purchased Fort Mott in order to add the land to the state's growing park system. It took four years to ready the site, which opened to the public on June 24, 1951, to great fanfare. Fort Mott as an army post had been transformed into the state's newest park. After the opening ceremony, a large boat regatta was held in the waters just off Fort Mott. Scores of visitors crowded the embankments that once hid the large guns. Fort Mott was now open and off to an exciting start.

In the years since it opened, Fort Mott State Park has seen many changes. Some of the buildings were lost due to fire, while others were sold to private owners and moved off park property. The post library and an officers' quarters were both sold and moved across the street from the park. These buildings still stand today and are both private residences. Some of the buildings that remained at the park also became private residences. When the state took over ownership of the land, the noncommissioned officers' quarters were used as rental properties. As when the land was an Army post, numerous families raised their children in these houses and used the grounds as their playground. The last tenant moved out in 2001.

Always a hub of activity, Fort Mott State Park has been the site of numerous reenactments, Boy Scout Camporees, and family reunions. Since its opening, the park has provided many recreational activities for visitors such as fishing, birding, and hiking. At one point, an Olympic-sized pool and a marina were contemplated. However, while recreational activities flourished, time began to take its toll on the historic buildings and fortifications. By the late 1980s, both fire control towers were closed to the public, and most of the gun batteries were dilapidated and inaccessible to the public.

Park employees had their work cut out for them as preparation began to open the park to the public. In the years since the Army abandoned the site, vegetation had overtaken the once manicured fort. In this photograph taken from the western fire control tower, all that is recognizable is the peace magazine and moat to the far left. (Fort Mott State Park.)

In this view from the Delaware River, the fields in front of the fortifications are completel overgrown. Controlled burns and bulldozers were required to finally remove all the brush an vegetation. (Fort Mott State Park.)

Taken immediately after a controlled burn of the brush on the embankment in front of Battery Harker and Battery Arnold, this photograph shows what a monumental undertaking it was to clear the grounds. (Fort Mott State Park.)

Roads once paved had been reduced to dirt, as shown in this 1947 photograph looking toward the parade ground. The post headquarters is visible to the right, while the ordnance warehouse is just visible on the left. (Fort Mott State Park.)

The western fire control tower, just visible above the tree line, still stands as a quiet sentinel over the old fort while Battery Arnold's Emplacement 1 shows the scars of being disarmed. The Killcohook Dredge Spoil Disposal area is seen in the background jutting out into the river. (Fort Mott State Park.)

Battery Arnold's Emplacement 1, stripped of its 12-inch gun, still shows the black asphalt paint applied to the gun deck and roof by the Army. The paint was used as a waterproofing agent to help keep the magazine below as dry as possible. (Fort Mott State Park.)

In this 1947 photograph of staff and visitors walking down Battery Lane, the wooden platforms that once connected all the gun decks of Battery Harker and Battery Arnold are sill present. The small building in the center right of the photograph was a storehouse for the gun emplacements. (Fort Mott State Park.)

A far cry from its former glory, Battery Arnold sits derelict. Prior to the park's opening, a local resident found an interesting use for the now dark and damp gun batteries—growing mushrooms. The Mott Mushroom Company rented the space from the state until the park opened to the public. (Fort Mott State Park.)

In preparation to open the park, all the grounds were re-graded and flattened. In this photograph, park employees run a pulvi-mixer behind a tractor to recondition the soil so that a new grass field could be planted. (Fort Mott State Park.)

In this photograph taken from the parados, a bulldozer sits waiting while the pulvi-mixer runs in the field. Countless hours were required to create a site that would be suitable for the public to enjoy. (Fort Mott State Park.)

On November 25, 1950, Fort Mott and the surrounding area were hit by a nor'easter that was later called the Great Appalachian Storm of 1950. Within three hours, most of the park grounds were covered by waist-deep water. In other parts of the state, the storm generated winds up to 108 miles per hour. This view down Battery Lane between the fortification and the parados shows the amount of water that covered the park. (Fort Mott State Park.)

In this view, the Delaware River reaches all the way to the guardhouse during the storm of November 1950. Due to the rising floodwaters, local residents around the park were evacuated from their homes, only to be forced to return when the bus sent to rescue them encountered water too deep to cross. (Fort Mott State Park.)

Back on the pulvi-mixer pulled by the park's John Deere tractor, park staff complete re-grading the fields around the park. The fields are ready to be seeded with grass and become the open space park visitors know today. (Fort Mott State Park.)

Almost ready for opening day ceremonies, the fortifications are now cleared of all unwanted vegetation. A new bathhouse sits in the field just past Battery Gregg. (Fort Mott State Park.)

Cleaned up with a fresh coat of whitewash and paint on the metal surfaces, Battery Arnold is ready for the park to be opened to the public. (Fort Mott State Park.)

The Department of Conservation and Economic Development's

Dedication of

FORT MOTT STATE PARK
AND BOAT REGATTA

Sponsored by

THE SERVICE MEN'S MEMORIAL HOME ASS'N.
PENNS GROVE, NEW JERSEY

SUNDAY, JUNE 24, 1951

On Sunday, June 24, 1951, Fort Mott State Park was officially dedicated as a park for the citizen of New Jersey to enjoy. Shown here is the cover of the official program of the event. (Fort Mot State Park.)

Dedication ceremonies were led by members of the Service Men's Memorial Home Association of Penns Grove, New Jersey. They are shown here raising the flag for the first time over the new park. After the flag was raised, Mrs. Jerome LaVine sang the national anthem. (Fort Mott State Park.)

The Honorable Charles R. Erdman Jr., New Jersey's commissioner of conservation and economic development, formally names and presents the park to the state. Erdman, a World War I veteran, headed the New Jersey Department of Conservation and Economic Development for five years and would also add Wharton State Forest to the park service during his tenure. (Fort Mott State Park.)

In this photograph of the dedication of the park, the Honorable John M. Summerill (right), state senator from Salem County, accepts Fort Mott State Park on behalf of the citizens of New Jersey. The ceremony was followed by a military drill provided by the Veterans of Foreign Wars of Quinton. (Fort Mott State Park.)

Providing the perfect vantage point for spectators, the embankments in front of Battery Arnold and Battery Harker were filled with visitors watching the Fort Mott Regatta on Sunday, June 24, 1951. (Fort Mott State Park.)

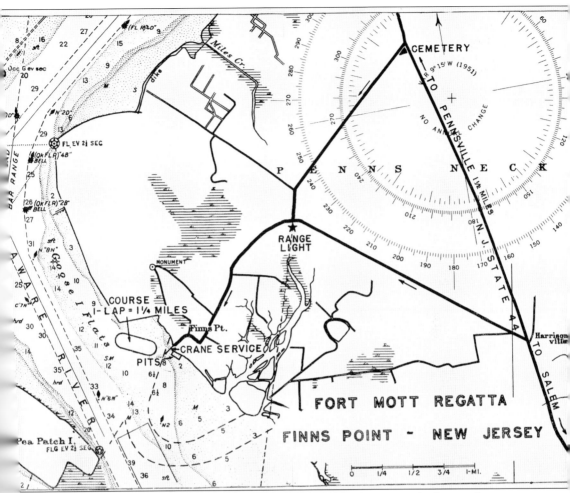

Immediately following the dedication ceremony, the Fort Mott Regatta took place in the waters of the Delaware River. The boating events were sponsored by the Penns Grove and Salem Boat Clubs. Events took place from 11:00 a.m. until 4:30 p.m., with boat crane service at the end of the wharf to put craft in the river. (Fort Mott State Park.)

The Fort Mott Regatta race officials as listed in the official program were Max Wallen (chief timer), Jack Geissingler (assistant timer), George Schock (chief starter), Ken Spigelmyer (assistant starter), Howard Zimmerman (measurer), Claude McFarland (race announcer), Harvey Bakley (chief scorer), Grover Young (pit manager), Roland Hann (gunner), John LeCarpentier (representing the Penns Grove Boat Club), and Edwin Powell (representing the Salem Boat Club). (Fort Mott State Park.)

Crowds line the seawall as well as the top of the batteries and even appear on the western fire control tower to get the best possible view of the racing watercraft on the first day Fort Mott State Park is open to the public. (Fort Mott State Park.)

Leapin Lena sits waiting to be placed in the water for the inboard hydroplane race during the Fort Mott Regatta on Sunday, June 24, 1951. Crowds in the background can be seen on the embankments of Battery Arnold and Battery Harker. (Fort Mott State Park.)

In this photograph, the Delaware River is teeming with activity as spectators watch the Fort Mott Regatta. The crane to place boats in the water is visible on the wharf. (Fort Mott State Park.)

This view shows cabin cruisers lining up to watch races of the Fort Mott Regatta on Sunday, June 24, 1951. During the race, the waters off of Fort Mott State Park were full of small watercraft. (Fort Mott State Park.)

Vehicles fill the original parking lot behind the ordnance warehouse on the park's opening day. Just out of view to the left is the picnic area and playground. (Fort Mott State Park.)

With a fresh coat of whitewash and trimmed grounds, the generating room, switchboard room, and Batteries Edwards and Krayenbuhl are ready for visitors. (Fort Mott State Park.)

An early visitor to Fort Mott State Park stops for a photograph on Battery Harker's Emplacement 2's gun deck. The guns of Battery Harker were removed in 1940, when they were sold to the Canadian government for use in the coastal defense of Newfoundland and the St. Lawrence Seaway. (Fort Mott State Park.)

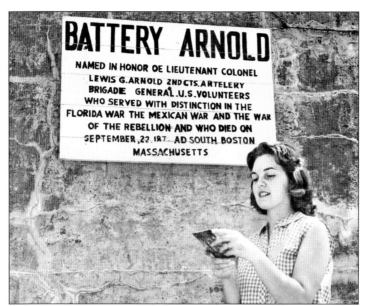

The same visitor to the park stops by one of the original interpretive signs outside of Battery Arnold. Hopefully, the visitor did not notice the spelling error. In the 1990s, interpretive signage would be placed throughout the fort. (Fort Mott State Park.)

Two visitors look inside an emplacement of Battery Arnold. No longer being painted yearly by Army personnel, the massive blast doors and barred doors have begun to show their age. The Army replaced the original wooden blast doors with the large steel doors visible in this photograph. (Fort Mott State Park.)

The picnic area was initially located close to the river, near where the moat emptied into the Delaware River. In this photograph, the western fire control tower and peace magazine are visible across the moat. (Fort Mott State Park.)

his photograph, taken from the western fire control tower, shows the park's original picnic ea, located near the river behind the guardhouse. Eventually, the picnic area and parking lot ere moved closer to the bathhouse, located by Battery Gregg on the other side of the park. ort Mott State Park.)

The old post headquarters sits vacant in 1963. For a short time, it was used as housing for the park's superintendent. The eastern fire control tower is visible to the right of the building. (Fort Mott State Park.)

The park's first maintenance area utilized existing buildings constructed by the Army. Th building at the center of this photograph was the stable for the mules that were used by th quartermaster to pull carts on the railway that led from the wharf to the peace magazine. (Fo Mott State Park.)

The maintenance shop and stable were destroyed by fire in the 1960s, and all that remained was the chimney and foundation. The building visible to the left would act as the maintenance shop until it also was claimed by fire in the 1970s. (Fort Mott State Park.)

In this view out of Battery Edwards's Emplacement 2, looking toward the river, a visitor can be seen walking the seawall. Battery Edwards's guns were specifically designed to fire from openings like the one pictured here. Originally a powder magazine in the 1870s, the structure was later modified to house a three-inch rapid-fire gun. (Fort Mott State Park.)

Fort Mott State Park has always been a place for quiet reflection. Two women sit on a bench on Battery Edwards and watch the ship traffic on the Delaware River. The northern end of Pea Patch Island is just visible on the left, while the Delaware City Getty Oil Refinery is seen on the right. (Fort Mott State Park.)

Fort Mott State Park's bathhouse was located in what is now the picnic area on the site of the current restroom. The bathhouse had a center pavilion and men's and women's restrooms on both ends of the pavilion. Later, because of the strong currents in the water around Fort Mott, swimming in that section of the Delaware was banned, and the bathhouse was reconfigured into a restroom and picnic pavilion. (Fort Mott State Park.)

In this photograph, three visitors are enjoying the park by riding horses in the fields in front of the fortifications. The bathhouse is visible in the background. The fields around the park have seen many activities throughout the years, from military reenactments to dog races to soccer tournaments, giving the public countless opportunities for recreational activities. (Fort Mott State Park.)

When the State of New Jersey purchased Fort Mott in 1947, all the remaining buildings were included with the purchase. Some of the buildings were immediately sold and moved off park property, while others, like these two noncommissioned officers' duplexes, were turned into tenant housing. The last tenant moved out in 2001, and the buildings are currently awaiting restoration. (Fort Mott State Park.)

An unlucky park visitor should have turned left instead of right, ending up in Battery Krayenbuhl's Emplacement 1 with his vehicle. Eventually a crane had to be used to remove the vehicle. (Fort Mott State Park.)

Standing to the rear of Battery Harker's Emplacement 3 and serving as Fort Mott's sole interpretive sign and bulletin board, this brick structure remained until the numerous interpretive signs of the current self-guided walking tour were installed in the mid-1990s. (Fort Mott State Park.)

An entrance to one of the powder magazines from the 1870s construction sits half-buried. This magazine was part of a larger plan calling for an 11-gun battery to be built on the site in the 1870s. The project was halted when funds ran out in 1876. Later, a fire control structure for Battery Edwards was built on top of the magazine. (Fort Mott State Park.)

For a short period of time, Division C of the New Jersey State Forest Fire Service kept a brush truck at Fort Mott State Park. In this photograph, the forest fire service's truck is pictured with a state park ranger's vehicle in front of Battery Gregg. (Fort Mott State Park.)

Maj. David Kirschbaum (USA ret.) staffs the park office at Fort Mott, which is located within the former guardhouse. Major Kirschbaum was a fixture at the park from the late 1980s until 2003, when he retired. (Fort Mott State Park.)

Five

REBIRTH AND RESTORATION

For many years, Fort Mott State Park was considered a park that had historic features on its grounds, rather than a historic site in its own right. By the late 1980s, the pendulum began to swing in the other direction. With the establishment of the New Jersey Coastal Heritage Trail and the restoration of the wharf, visitor attendance at the park increased and Fort Mott State Park's historical importance began to be recognized, along with the need to restore the site's historic structures. With employees like Paul Taylor in the New Jersey Office of Historic Sites and Chief Ranger Bruce Mathews at Fort Mott State Park spearheading the initial push for restoration, changes began to happen at the once-sleepy state park.

Chief Ranger Bruce Mathews inspects the interior of Battery Edwards in the early 1990s. The structure that contains this emplacement was a gunpowder magazine in the 1870s construction. In the 1890s construction, the Army repurposed the magazine to create a casemate in which specially modified three-inch guns could be mounted. (Fort Mott State Park.)

Congressman William Hughes speaks at the opening of the New Jersey Coastal Heritage Trai Delsea Region's Welcome Center from the porch of the guardhouse. The welcome center wa built within the fort's ordnance warehouse. (Fort Mott State Park.)

To help improve visitors' experience to the historic fort, a self-guided walking tour with interpretive signs was placed throughout the fortifications and around the park. In this photograph, William "Tubby" Watterson and his wife, Mary Watterson Clement (left), stand in front of one of the interpretive signs to which they contributed photographs and information. (Fort Mott State Park.)

Interpretive signage was placed at numerous points along the walking tour of the fortifications. Here, a worker is preparing to install a sign in the square communication niche located on the wall of the gun deck. This sign describes the different types of communication equipment once employed at the fort. (Fort Mott State Park.)

Once almost totally reclaimed by the Delaware River, the wharf is back in working order. With the restoration project completed, transportation between the three forts was available for the first time since the Army abandoned the site. In 1997, the Three Forts Ferry began service between Fort Mott, Fort Delaware, and Delaware City. (Fort Mott State Park.)

New Jersey governor Christine Todd Whitman stops to pose for a photograph while on an official visit to Fort Mott State Park. Governor Whitman later took the ferry to Fort Delaware on Pea Patch Island to meet with Gov. Thomas Carper of Delaware. (Fort Mott State Park.)

In the mid-1990s, the park's first major restoration project was the repair of Battery Gregg's concrete. In this photograph, new landscaping matting is put down to help control soil erosion around the battery. Prior to the restoration, the battery was fenced off and closed to the public. Now, the battery is the beginning of the walking tour. (Fort Mott State Park.)

In 1999, the exterior of the post headquarters underwent major restoration. As part of the project, sections of the clapboard had to be completely replaced because of water damage. This rear view of the building shows the extent of the project. At the front of the building, the porch was also rebuilt. (Fort Mott State Park.)

In 2003, the two-story, glass-topped tower was dismantled so it could undergo restoration. In this photograph, the two-story cabin is being lifted off the steel superstructure. In the years leading up to the restoration, the tower had been closed to the public. (Fort Mott State Park.)

With a new glass roof, rebuilt floor, and a new steel superstructure to sit upon, the cabin is ready to be lifted back onto its perch. Currently, Fort Mott's tower is the only example of the two-story, glass-topped tower that the public can enter. (Fort Mott State Park.)

Charles Dougherty (left) and his brother Jeffery volunteer during an event at the park. Fort Mott relies on many volunteers to help with interpretive programming and projects. The passion and dedication of the volunteers is evidenced in the quality of interpretation and work they provide at the site. (Fort Mott State Park.)

During a living history event, Rick Stauber talks to a group of children about the large disappearing guns once emplaced at Battery Arnold. Interpretive groups like the Army Ground Forces Association have helped to bring the site back to life. (Fort Mott State Park.)

Park staff don period uniforms for the first living history event in which the two-story fire control tower is open. Filled with period equipment, the tower provides the public with greater insight into why Fort Mott was important to the defense of the Delaware River. Shown here are, from left to right, Andy Grant, Mike Bonaccorsi, Larry Winchell IV, and Stephen Turner Jr. (Fort Mott State Park.)

Members of the Army Ground Forces Association and park staff stand at attention during a living history event. During this event, the change of unit from the 7th Coast Artillery to the 21st Coast Artillery in 1940 was reenacted. Pictured here are, from left to right, Gary Weaver, Stephen Turner Jr., Larry Winchell IV, Peter Morrill, Mike Bonaccorsi, and Thomas Minton. (Fort Mott State Park.)

Pat Peters (third from right) and John Houck (right) of the Salem Light Artillery help visitor Jesse Lebovics demonstrate the firing of a Civil War Williams gun. Over the years, many living history events have included cannon fire and weapon demonstrations. (Fort Mott State Park.)

The interior of the post headquarters is well on its way to being restored, as seen in this interior photograph taken from the staircase. At some point in the 1950s, the interior walls were stripped to their studs and the original tin ceilings were taken down. Vacant and unused until the restoration, the building is now used for interpretive displays. (Fort Mott State Park.)

Wood trim awaits installation during the interior restoration of the post headquarters. Because most of the original wood trim was missing, a large quantity of trim had to be specially fabricated to match the existing woodwork. With the project complete, the post headquarters appears as it did in the early 1900s. (Fort Mott State Park.)

In 1904, the Army built the peace magazine to hold gunpowder and to keep it dry. In April 2006, the magazine, the last remaining example of this type of building constructed by the Army, caught fire. The fire was so hot that the granite lintels over the doorways cracked, and the fire relit multiple times the next day after being put out. (Fort Mott State Park.)

Mike Neicen inspects what is left amid the complete and utter destruction following the fire of the peace magazine. Because the building was designed to be highly ventilated, many wooden artifacts were stored inside. The fire reduced everything made out of wood into charcoal. (Fort Mott State Park.)

In this photograph, restoration of the peace magazine is well under way. With the brick walls stabilized, specially milled wood was brought in so the building could be restored to its original character and configuration. When the restoration was complete, the building appeared as it did when built in 1904. (Fort Mott State Park.)

Shawn (left) and Adam Welch help to restore a BD-74 fire control switchboard. Recovered from Fort H.G. Wright on Fisher's Island, New York, the telephone switchboard required a complete rewiring. Over 1,500 solder points, hundreds of feet of wire, and countless hours went into the restoration. This is the only known functional BD-74, now used as an interpretive device at the park. (Fort Mott State Park.)

Larry Winchell IV (left) looks on as Adam Welch solders contacts on the BD-74 fire control switchboard. The switchboard, from the 1930s, required extensive restoration and had to be completely rewired. The original wire within the switchboard was covered in paper wrapping that had either disintegrated or become extremely fragile. (Fort Mott State Park.)

In this 2008 photograph, participants in the park's "School of the Soldier" program stand in formation for their graduation. During this weekend event, the children were taught many of the skills that the soldiers at Fort Mott would have learned when they entered the service. Marching, facing movements, and manual of arms were just a few things that were introduced to these fresh recruits. (Fort Mott State Park.)

Searchlights were part of the harbor defenses of the Delaware River, and when the Army was stationed at Fort Mott, it used one to illuminate the river. In 2007, Fort Mott once again took possession of a carbon arc searchlight. In this photograph, superintendent Vince Bonica (center) and maintenance supervisor Mike Neicen accept delivery from Jack Doehr (left) of a 1942 Sperry searchlight. (Fort Mott State Park.)

Preparing to illuminate the night sky in 2011, Vince Turner (left), Andy Grant (center), an Chris Simich complete a final check of the searchlight before striking the arc. The 60-inc searchlight emits a beam that is 800 million candlepower and can shine up to 30,000 feet int the heavens. (Chris Zeeman Collection.)

Members of the 9th Division Historical Preservation Society ride in the back of a 1941 GMC 2.5-ton truck during a reenactment. In recent years, Fort Mott has become home of the Historic Soldiers Weekend event, which highlights military history and honors veterans. (Fort Mott State Park.)

Battery Arnold's Emplacement 1 is seen here undergoing a major face lift. Phase one of a multiphase project to rehabilitate the concrete called for the removal and replacement of all loose concrete on the exterior of the emplacement. (Fort Mott State Park.)

Now complete, the exterior restoration of Battery Arnold's Emplacement 1 has returned the site to the way it would have looked prior to the installation of the 12-inch disappearing gun in 1896. The large counterweight well is now open, allowing visitors a more complete view of the emplacement's original design. (Fort Mott State Park.)

Six

FINNS POINT
NATIONAL CEMETERY

Finns Point National Cemetery lies just over half a mile northwest of the flagpole on Fort Mott's parade ground. The cemetery was originally part of the Fort Mott Military Reservation but was retained by the federal government when Fort Mott was put up for sale in 1947. Still an active cemetery, Finns Point is best known as the final resting place of 2,436 Confederate soldiers who died while imprisoned on Pea Patch Island during the Civil War. These men are memorialized in an 85-foot-tall obelisk monument to the Confederate dead that was constructed in 1910. Set aside as a cemetery in 1863, the site was dedicated as a national cemetery on October 3, 1875. The monument to the Union guards who died while on duty at Fort Delaware was constructed in 1879. Finns Point National Cemetery is also the final resting place of 13 soldiers who fought for the German army and passed away while being held as prisoners of war at Fort Dix, New Jersey. Many of the older graves in the cemetery are marked with the distinctive white marble headstones, while the post–World War II graves lie flush with the ground.

Located on the cemetery grounds is a Meigs Lodge, built in the 1870s. Designed in the Second Empire style with a mansard roof to house the cemetery's superintendent, the one-and-a-half-story structure provided administration space and accommodations for the superintendent's family until the late 1980s. A later addition to the structure gave the occupants a kitchen, which had previously been located in another building. When Fort Mott was owned by the Army, a soldier from the fort would regularly be assigned to help with maintenance projects at the cemetery. The current wall surrounding the cemetery was extended during the 1930s and early 1940s with the help of the Works Project Administration and soldiers from Fort Mott. When first established, the cemetery sat on the banks of the Delaware River. Today, as a result of the depositing of dredge spoils on the banks of the Delaware, the cemetery is more than half a mile from the river and surrounded by salt marsh. In 1978, the cemetery was added to the National Register of Historic Places.

Today, regular ceremonies on Memorial Day, Veterans Day, and, recently, the Wreath Across America program, demonstrate that these servicemen and servicewomen are not forgotten.

This 1906 photograph shows the stone wall and entrance to Finns Point National Cemetery. Prior to the construction of the granite obelisk to memorialize the Confederate prisoners of war who perished while imprisoned at Fort Delaware, the only monument to those who died and were buried at the cemetery during the Civil War was for the 150 Union guards who passed away at Fort Delaware. In 1910, a monument to mark the graves of the 2,436 Confederate dead was erected. (A. Grant Collection.)

The Grant family from Woodstown, New Jersey, visits the cemetery in the early 1920s. Until the latter half of the 20th century, trees were abundant in the cemetery, as can be seen behind the monument. (A. Grant Collection.)

IN MEMORY   STARVED CONFEDERATES   FINNS POINT N.J. NAT'L CEMETERY

The 85-foot-high monument for the Confederate dead was erected in 1910 by an act of federal legislation. The law also authorized marking the graves of Confederate soldiers who died while in federal prisons and military hospitals and were buried in the North. (A. Grant Collection.)

During a Memorial Day observance, reenactors place wreaths on the monument to the Union guards who passed away while stationed at Fort Delaware during the Civil War. The cupola surrounding the monument was erected in the 1930s. (Fort Mott State Park.)

Reenactors hold a ceremony on Memorial Day at the Confederate Monument at Finns Point National Cemetery. Every Memorial Day, reenactors come to the cemetery to pay tribute to those who served their country. (Fort Mott State Park.)

World War II reenactors make their way to the 2011 Wreaths Across America ceremony at Finns Point National Cemetery in the back of a 1941 GMC CCKW 2.5-ton truck. (Jane Turner Collection.)

reenactors prepare to raise the flag at the Wreaths Across America ceremony at Finns Point ational Cemetery. Shown here are, from left to right, an unidentified Civil War reenactor, nce Turner II, Vince Turner, Gary Weaver, and Gary Oprendek. (Jane Turner Collection.)

Civil War Union soldier reenactors place wreaths during Wreaths Across America. The nationally organized ceremony, featuring wreath-laying on the same day in December, remembers and honors veterans. (Jane Turner Collection.)

The Union Monument is adorned with wreaths during a Wreaths Across America ceremony. Hundreds of wreaths were laid upon all of the graves located at Finns Point National Cemetery. All of the wreaths were sponsored by local residents. (Jane Turner Collection.)

Not all of the graves at Finns Point National Cemetery are of veterans. One section was reserved for families of soldiers stationed at Fort Mott and other military sites. This photograph of the "Post Section," next to the caretaker's quarters, shows wreaths that were recently placed. (Jane Turner Collection.)

Finns Point National Cemetery is the final resting place of 13 German prisoners of war who died while interned at Fort Dix, New Jersey, during World War II. This photograph shows two gravestones of German prisoners of war. (Jane Turner Collection.)

A silent sentinel and testament to the importance of the Delaware River as a means of transportation, the Finns Point Rear Range Light stands on the end of Lighthouse Road, a mile inland from Fort Mott. Rising 115 feet into the air, the tower once housed a kerosene vapor light with a catadiotric lens that could create a 150,000-candlepower beam. When the shipping channel was changed in 1950, the light, considered obsolete, was extinguished. (Fort Mott State Park.)

In this period postcard, the Finns Point Rear Range Light stands at the fork of the road between Fort Mott to the right and Pigs Eye (Harrisonville) to the left. Built in 1877 of wrought iron by the Kellogg Bridge Company of Buffalo, New York, the light began operation on April 2, 1877. (Stephen Turner Jr. Collection.)

Finn's Point light, Pennsville, N. J.

Finns Point front from N. W. 175

The Finns Point Front Range Light once sat on the banks of the Delaware River, south of Fort Mott. The structure consisted of a one-and-a-half-story wood frame building with the light accessible from the second story. This rare photograph shows the light from the northwest and the surrounding land that the keeper used to raise livestock. Prone to flooding and storm damage, the building was torn down in 1939. (National Archives.)

In this 1936 Signal Corps aerial photograph of Fort Mott, the fortifications are visible to the left, with Battery Gregg partially obscured by trees at the bottom. The guns of Battery Harker and Battery Arnold can be clearly seen in the firing position as they are being maintained by the caretakers assigned to Fort Mott. A handful of soldiers were assigned to the fort to maintain the guns in case they were ever called back into action. When this photograph was taken, it had been 14 years since the main garrison of troops left Fort Mott, and many trees and bushes can be seen growing in front of the gun line. The areas where three of the large officers' quarters once stood now appear as dirt patches to the lower right of the image. One of the barracks buildings which would be torn down later in the year, still stands on the parade ground on the right (National Archives.)

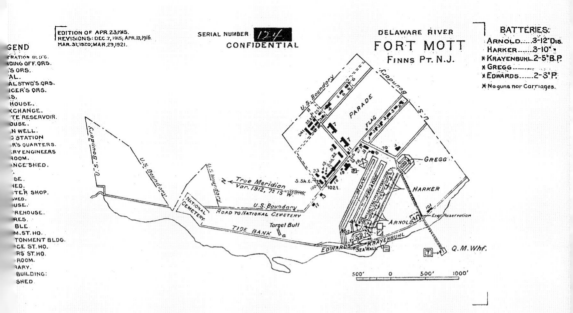

This 1915 map, revised in 1921, illustrates the layout of Fort Mott, New Jersey. The locations of the batteries and the buildings as well as the roads that once crisscrossed the post can be seen on the map. Today, only six of the buildings depicted here still stand in Fort Mott State Park. The map also shows the original location of the banks of the Delaware River and the location of Finns Point National Cemetery. Later, with the creation of the Killcohook Dredge Disposal Area, the topography of the area changed greatly; the cemetery is now located over a half-mile from the shores of the Delaware River. When the State of New Jersey purchased Fort Mott for $14,000 in 1947, the national cemetery was retained as federal property. (National Archives.)

DISCOVER THOUSANDS OF LOCAL HISTORY BOOKS FEATURING MILLIONS OF VINTAGE IMAGES

Arcadia Publishing, the leading local history publisher in the United States, is committed to making history accessible and meaningful through publishing books that celebrate and preserve the heritage of America's people and places.

Find more books like this at
www.arcadiapublishing.com

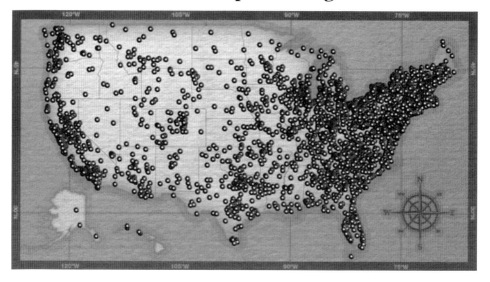

Search for your hometown history, your old stomping grounds, and even your favorite sports team.

Consistent with our mission to preserve history on a local level, this book was printed in South Carolina on American-made paper and manufactured entirely in the United States. Products carrying the accredited Forest Stewardship Council (FSC) label are printed on 100 percent FSC-certified paper.

MADE IN THE USA